EVE...
MAD...™

KT-158-801

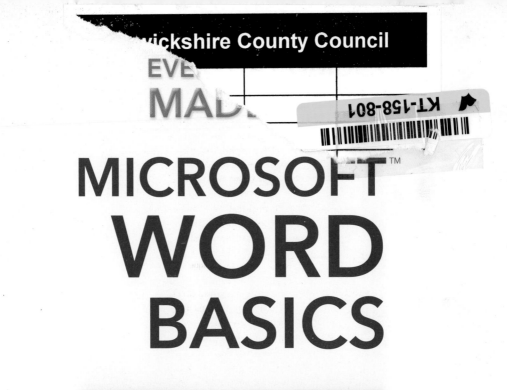

MICROSOFT
WORD
BASICS

This is a **FLAME TREE** book
First published 2014

Publisher and Creative Director: Nick Wells
Project Editor: Catherine Taylor
Art Director and Layout Design: Mike Spender
Digital Design and Production: Chris Herbert
Copy Editor: Anna Groves
Screenshots: Roger Laing
Original Text: Rob Hawkins
Proofreader: Dawn Laker
Indexer: Helen Snaith

Special thanks to: Monique Jensen

This edition first published 2014 by
FLAME TREE PUBLISHING
Crabtree Hall, Crabtree Lane
Fulham, London SW6 6TY
United Kingdom

www.flametreepublishing.com

© 2014 Flame Tree Publishing

ISBN 978-1-78361-390-8

A CIP record for this book is available from the British Library upon request.

Printed in China

All *non*-screenshot pictures are courtesy of Shutterstock.com and © the following photographers: soliman design 1 & 8; Antonov Roman 3 & 92; Dragon Images 5; Dean Drobot 10; Syda Productions 12; wavebreakmedia 14; racorn 24, 56t; jannoon028 25; bikeriderlondon 32, 74; matka_Wariatka 34; wrangler 35; Dragon Images 38, 68; KieferPix 40; marekuliasz 43; Tyler Olson 46t; Pressmaster 47; deckard_73 57; B Calkins 60; Sergey Mironov 82; Thinglass 84; Monkey Business Images 91b; Ammentorp Photography 96; clarkfang 98; Nata-lia 101; Jerome Scholler 106t; dotshock 110; LittleStocker 116; Eugenio Marongiu 118b; rangizzz 120b.

EVERYDAY GUIDES
MADE EASY

MICROSOFT™
WORD
BASICS

ROGER LAING

SERIES FOREWORD BY MARK MAYNE

FLAME TREE
PUBLISHING

CONTENTS

Get started with no-nonsense instructions on finding and opening files,
saving work and moving around a document.

Discover quick techniques for creating documents, selecting and copying text,
changing views and printing.

Here's how to save time when creating and editing a document and fix any likely problems.

Follow our step-by-step techniques, including creating a poster and a letterhead.

Time to customize Word and see how to protect your documents, edit images,
print on envelopes and more.

See how to use mobile apps for tablets and smartphones, and Word Online,
to create and edit your documents.

SERIES FOREWORD

Windows, launched in 1985, began as a way to navigate PCs without having to resort to command prompts, and, although early versions might look clunky by today's standards, the concept of navigating a computer through 'windows' rather than through hard-to-remember commands immediately caught on. Millions of installs later, Windows is the most popular computer operating system on the planet, with more than 1.25 billion PCs running a version of Windows today.

To complement Windows in the business space, Microsoft developed Microsoft Office back in 1990, and without Office programs like Word, Excel and Powerpoint our world would look very different today.

This guide on Microsoft Word is designed to take you from zero to hero without any of the pain, but fear not, we won't bamboozle you with jargon. We'll mainly cover the basics of this feature-rich software, progressing through to some advanced functions and finally troubleshooting. Each chapter has a number of Hot Tips that'll ensure you're on the very cutting edge without lifting a finger.

This step-by-step guide is written by an acknowledged expert on Word, so you can be sure of the best advice, and is suitable for anyone from the complete beginner through to slightly more advanced users who would like a refresher. You'll find this guide an excellent reference volume on Word, and it will grace your bookcase for years to come.

Mark Mayne
Editor of T3.com

INTRODUCTION

Microsoft Word first appeared over 30 years ago. Since then, this computerized typewriter has evolved with an increasing number of features that can be very confusing for the beginner. This book explains it all.

NEED TO KNOW

Filled with practical advice, this book will guide you through the basics of Word, as well as some of the more advanced features – such as AutoCorrect or Image Editing – to help you become more proficient.

SMALL CHUNKS

Every chapter has short paragraphs describing particular features within Word and how to use them. They don't have to be read in order, just dip into individual sections as needed.

STEP-BY-STEP GUIDES

These provide clear and concise instructions on using Word for a variety of tasks, from creating a leaflet to a poster for an event.

SIX CHAPTERS

This book is split into six chapters. The first explains the jargon used in Word and gets you started opening, closing and navigating documents. The second chapter covers quick and easy techniques for creating documents, handling text, changing views and printing. Chapter three has useful timesavers and helps fix any problems. Chapter four shows how you can use Word for projects, such as creating a poster or setting up a letterhead. Chapter five covers some of the more advanced features in Word. Finally, in Chapter six discover how you can use Word Online from any computer and the mobile apps available for tablets and smartphones.

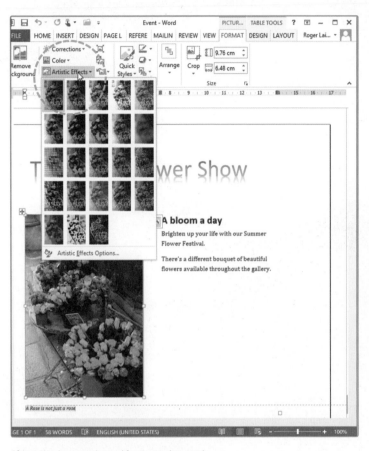

Above: Word can even be used for image editing, such as adding artistic effects by using the picture tools.

Hot Tips

Look out for the Hot Tips, which tell you about the many shortcuts and quick techniques available in Word.

ALL ABOUT WORD

WHAT IS A WORD PROCESSOR?

A word processor is the computer equivalent of a typewriter, but with many more features that can save time and reduce mistakes. The following pages outline how the word processor and Microsoft Word have evolved.

WORD PROCESSOR EVOLUTION

The word processor was designed along the lines of the typewriter and evolved accordingly. Early versions used typewriter features, still available today, including tabs and line spacing.

WYSIWYG

One of the most essential developments in word processing was to ensure that the layout and the style of the words on the screen would look exactly the same when printed. This is known as WYSIWYG, which stands for What You See Is What You Get. Nowadays, we take this for granted, but during the 1980s, many word processors did not offer this feature.

WORD VERSIONS

The origins of Microsoft Word can be traced back to 1983. The current version is Word 2013, which is available by subscription for the PC (Word 2011 for the Mac). It is part of Office 365, which includes other Microsoft programs, including Excel (for spreadsheets) and Outlook (for emails). There are various options available.

Subscription Services

- **Office 365 Personal**: This lets you install Word and the other programs on a single computer and one tablet for a monthly or annual subscription.

- **Office 365 Home**: Where a monthly or annual subscription lets you install Word and the other programs on up to five

Above: With WYSIWYG, you can be sure that what you have on your screen will be what you have on paper after printing.

Above: Having all your Office needs gathered in one place makes for easy access.

Above: The different Word Templates all available with Word on the iPad.

desktops or laptops (PC and Mac). In addition, you can install it on up to five tablets, such as Apple's iPad and Microsoft Surface.

- **Office 365 for Business**: Includes Microsoft Word plus a wider range of business applications.

Standalone Versions

There are also desktop versions of Word, for which you pay a one-off fee for the program. Word 2013 is the latest for the PC, Word 2011 for the Mac. See pages 19–23 to see the similarities and differences onscreen between the PC and Mac versions.

Mobile Versions

- **Tablets**: Touch-friendly apps let you view, create, edit and print your Word documents on the go.

- **Smartphones**: Preloaded on Windows smartphones, there are now Office apps for the iPhone and some Android phones that let you work with your Word documents.

Looking for

Panda

Lorem ipsum dolor sit amet, consectetuer adipiscing elit. Nulla justo. Phasellus quis justo in est hendrerit blandit. Quisque ante lorem, sagittis sagittis, vestibulum vitae, nonummy eget, turpis. Vestibulum eros urna, malesuada sit amet, vehicula dapibus.

Above: Taking Word with you on iPhone or Android makes working on the go much faster.

Office Online: Has pared-down versions of the Office programs, including Word, so you can make changes to your documents stored in OneDrive (see below). As it works in your web browser, you can use it from any PC.

Linked by the Cloud

The different versions of Word for your PC, tablet and smartphone let you work on your files wherever you are. To achieve this, Word lets you save and share your files in the Cloud – or, more precisely, in OneDrive. This is free, online storage space where you can save your files and sync them to any of your devices. You can sign up for your OneDrive account at www.onedrive.com

Below: With OneDrive, you can be sure you have access to your documents, even when away from your server.

Hot Tip

While all OneDrive accounts include some free storage space, up to 1 terabyte (TB) per user is available with Office 365 subscriptions.

WORD JARGON

Word processor programs have a vast assortment of technical terms, which can be confusing if you don't know what they mean. This section lists and defines some of the most commonly used terminology.

AUTOCORRECT

Word automatically corrects spelling mistakes (Autocorrect is switched on by default).

AUTOTEXT

This is text that can be instantly entered into a document without having to type all of it. It saves time on typing and is useful for text ranging from a few words to whole paragraphs.

BOOKMARK

Specific points in a document can be labelled as bookmarks. This makes it quicker to find places in a document.

DOCUMENT

A document in Word is a file containing one or more pages. The document is saved with a filename, followed by the extension .docx (.doc in earlier versions).

Below: An open document.

FOOTNOTE

Nonfiction books often use notes at the bottom of the page, which refer to particular points in the text. These are known as footnotes and can be created in Microsoft Word.

HEADINGS

Word uses a numbered system for headings. This is useful for creating a hierarchical structure – Heading 1 could be a chapter heading, whereas Heading 3 might be a subheading. Each heading is known as a style.

Above: Using headings styles will make your Word document look professional without fuss.

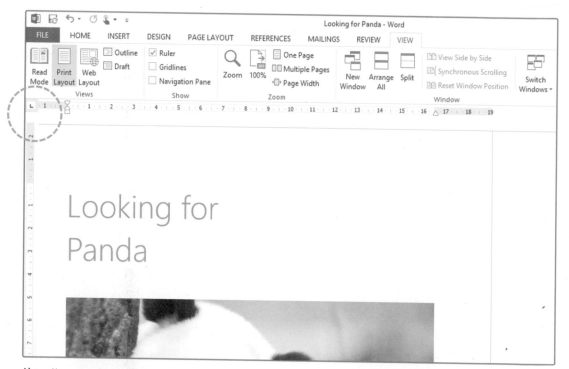

Above: You can see the ruler along the top and left of the page.

MARGINS

The space at the top, bottom, left and right of a page, between the edge of the text and the edge of the page.

RULER

A ruler can be displayed along the top of a page and down the left-hand side. This helps to work out how much space has been used on a page and is especially useful for tables and columns of text.

Hot Tip

The margins determine how close to the edge of a page the text is displayed and printed. The amount of space is measured in centimetres or inches and can be changed.

PAGE BREAK

When a new page is started in a document, this is technically known as a page break. A new page or page break starts when the text has filled the current page, or a page break can be purposely inserted.

SECTION BREAK

If a document uses particular fonts, colours or page layouts (for example, landscape A4) in one part and different settings in another, these formatting and page setup details can be separated with a section break.

STYLE

A style represents the details applied to text, such as the font type, size and colour and whether italic or bold is used. Preset styles include Normal for the main text in a document, Heading 1 and Heading 2 for a main heading and subheading, and Hyperlink for a website address. Using styles ensures the formatting is the same for particular types of text throughout a document. Preset styles are available, but you can also make your own.

TAB

Tabs are preset spaces between text, useful for creating multiple lists on a page. Tabs are a traditional feature of typewriters, but have been replaced in many cases by tables, which are easier to use.

TEMPLATE

This is a pre-created document that can be reused without destroying the original. This is ideal for saving time on typing and can be used for letters, faxes and leaflets.

THE WORD WINDOW

The main screen in Word can seem bewildering if you don't know what you're looking for and don't recognize any of the symbols on it. The following pages provide detailed explanations of the various aspects of the Word screen.

WORD 2013 ON THE PC

The screen looks very different to early versions of Word, with the menu bar replaced by a tabbed Ribbon system. As it's context-sensitive, the options available change according to the tab you're viewing.

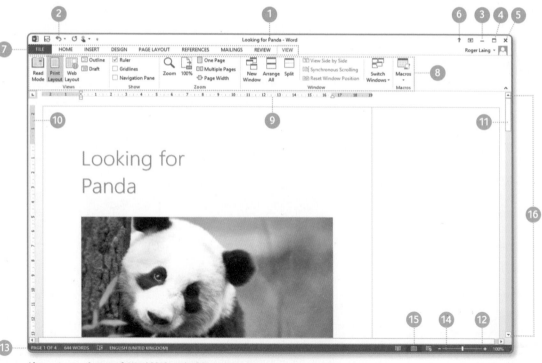

Above: A view of Microsoft Word 2013 on the PC.

① Title bar: The title bar appears at the top of all Microsoft applications. It displays the name of the application and current document.

② Quick Access Toolbar: Usually in the top-left corner of the screen, it can be moved further down, below the Ribbon. It displays some of the commonly used buttons, such as Open, Save, Undo and Quick Print. Buttons can be added and removed by clicking on its drop-down arrow.

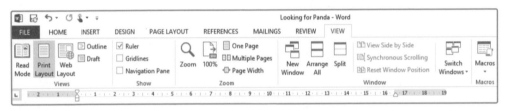

Above: A close-up view of the Quick Access Toolbar, which is above the Ribbon here.

Below: Search for solutions to your Word problems in the Word Help window.

③ Minimize button: Click on this button to hide the Word window and display whatever is behind it (another Word document if more are open). The document can be retrieved by clicking on its icon on the taskbar at the bottom of the screen.

④ Maximize/Restore button: If this button shows a single box, then clicking on it will enlarge the Word page to fill the screen (maximize). If two boxes are shown (Restore Down), then clicking it will reduce the page size.

⑤ Close button: Click on this to close the Word document that is displayed onscreen. If there are more Word documents open, these will remain open.

⑥ Help: Activates help window for information on using Word.

(7) Ribbon tabs: Near the top of the screen, these are labelled File, Home, Insert, Design, Page Layout, References, Mailings, Review and View. Click on each one to see various Word features that are grouped together into logically similar tasks, for example changing font size and colour on the Home tab.

(8) Ribbon: Contains a series of buttons, just like a traditional toolbar, to control the different features in Word.

(9) Horizontal ruler: Displays the horizontal dimensions (width) of the document in inches or centimetres.

(10) Vertical ruler: Displays the vertical dimensions (height) of a page in inches or centimetres.

(11) Vertical scroll bar: Used to scroll up and down a document.

> **Hot Tip**
>
> The Ribbon can be minimized by double-clicking the tab name. Double-click again to restore it.

Above: Minimizing your Ribbon is easily done, and can easily be reversed when needed.

(12) Horizontal scroll bar: Only displayed when the entire width of a page is too wide to be displayed on the screen. Provides left and right scrolling across the document.

Above: Page and word counts are visible on the status bar, along with which language is being used.

⑬ Status bar: Displays the number of pages and the word count for all the text. If only some text is selected, it displays that selection's word count.

⑭ Zoom control: Drag the slider left or right to zoom in and out, or click on the + and – symbols. Click on the percentage value to open a Zoom dialogue box and change the settings.

⑮ Layouts: Click on the small buttons to change to different views of the document, including Read Mode, Print Layout and Web Layout.

⑯ Vertical scroll buttons: Scrolls up and down slowly; or on the Mac scrolls one page at a time.

Hot Tip

You can split or divide the window vertically to view two areas of the document at the same time. Position the scroll bar where you want the divide, select the View tab and press the Split button.

Above: 'Split' enables you to view two areas of the document at the same time.

WORD ON MACS

Microsoft has developed Word to work in much the same way on Apple Macintosh computers as it does on a Windows platform. As seen in this picture of the latest standalone version – Word 2011 – the layout is similar. The numbers shown here correspond with the descriptions on pages 20–22.

Above: A view of Microsoft Word 2011 on the Mac.

KEYBOARD DIFFERENCES ON MACS

Any keyboard-related instructions in this book are based on using a PC keyboard, but – even if you are using a PC – depending on the type of keyboard you are using, you may find some differences. Similarly, if you are using an Apple Mac, there are a few different keys. For example, the 'Command' (⌘/⌥) key on the Mac has the same functions as the 'Ctrl' key on the PC (while the key labelled 'Ctrl' acts as the 'right-click'). The Page up/down keys on the Mac are usually labelled by an up/down arrow with two short horizontal lines. And, on *older* Mac mice, in order to 'right-click', hold down the Ctrl key and click, instead.

GETTING STARTED IN WORD

There are lots of shortcuts and quick techniques for opening, closing and saving Word documents and making sure files are not lost.

OPENING AND CLOSING WORD

There are no right or wrong methods, so it's worth experimenting to see which you find is quickest and easiest.

Opening Word

- **Windows 8.1**: In Modern View, double-click the icon for Word 2013. If you prefer to work in traditional Desktop Mode, right-click the Word 2013 icon and select Pin to Taskbar.

- **Taskbar**: Once pinned to the Taskbar, you'll see the Word blue icon (symbol) near the bottom left of the screen. Click this to open the program.

Above: Word can be opened via its icon on the Taskbar.

- **Open a Word document**: Instead of opening Word, you can open a Word document (also known as a file), which will automatically open the program. Word documents are usually found in your Documents folder.

- **Keyboard shortcut**: Some keyboards have a Microsoft Word symbol on one of the function keys (for example F2, as in the picture here), which opens the program. You may have to hold down another key on the keyboard (e.g. shift) to activate these keyboard features.

Below: Some keyboards have a Microsoft Word symbol on a particular key, which can be used to open the program.

Check Word Is Open

Not sure if Word is open or not? In Desktop Mode, look along the Taskbar at the bottom of the screen to see if it's displayed. If so, click on it to display the program onscreen.

Closing Word

○ **File menu:** Click the File tab on the Ribbon in Word, then select Close. If you have not saved any Word documents, you will be prompted to do so before the program closes.

○ **File menu using the keyboard:** Hold down the Alt key on the keyboard, then press F, followed by C for Close.

○ **Close button:** Click the X in the far top-right corner of the screen. If other Word windows are open, it will only close that Word document, otherwise the program will shut down.

○ **Keyboard shortcut:** Hold down the Alt key and press the F4 key.

○ **Right-click the Word icon on the taskbar:** Choose Close from the menu that appears.

Right: The X in the far top-right corner of the screen will close your document.

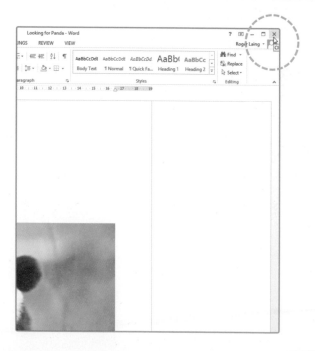

> ### Hot Tip
>
> If you have several programs open and are about to switch off – and you've saved your documents – just click on the Start button and choose **Turn Off Computer or Shut Down.**

OPENING NEW AND OLD WORD DOCUMENTS

Microsoft Word documents or files can be opened and created in a variety of ways via the keyboard, menus, toolbar buttons or a different program.

Creating a New Blank Word Document

- **Keyboard:** Hold down the Ctrl key on the keyboard, then press the letter N. A new Word document (file) will appear onscreen.

- **Ribbon:** Click the File tab on the Ribbon and choose New from the menu on the left. A variety of options will appear on the screen. Select Blank document to open a new document.

Below: Templates for every occasion can be found when opening a new document.

Opening a Recently Used Word Document

○ **Ribbon:** Click the File tab, then Open to see a list of the files last used in Word displayed in the main part of the screen. Select one to open it.

○ **Taskbar:** With Word open, right-click its icon on the Taskbar along the bottom of the screen. A menu will appear showing recent Word documents.

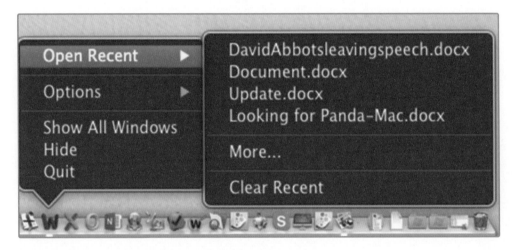

Above: Using the Taskbar to find recent documents with Word on a Mac.

Opening an Old Word Document

The following list shows different methods for accessing the Open dialogue box in Word to locate a document and open it.

○ **Keyboard shortcut:** Hold down the Ctrl key on the keyboard and press the letter O (not the zero). The Open dialogue box will appear on the screen.

○ **Ribbon:** Click the File tab on the Ribbon and choose Open.

● **Quick Access Toolbar**: If a yellow-coloured folder is displayed at the top of the Word window, click it to access the Open dialogue box. If there is no toolbar button, click the drop-down button beside the Quick Access Toolbar and choose Open from the menu that appears (see below).

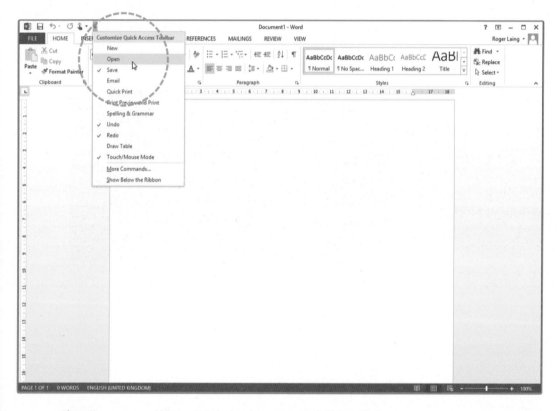

Above: You can open an old document via the drop-down menu on the Quick Access Toolbar.

Using Windows File Explorer to Open Word Documents
Open Windows File Explorer in Desktop Mode and click on Documents. Any Word document can be opened from here without having to open the program first.

SAVING

Save your work, don't lose it. It's good practice to regularly save your Word documents, but if a computer problem occurs, Word has some recovery methods to ensure all is not lost.

Saving a Word Document for the First Time

If you are working on a new Word document, which hasn't been saved before, then you will need to save and name it. The quickest way to do this is to hold down the Ctrl key on the keyboard and press the letter S. A Save As dialogue box will appear. Enter a name for the document and choose a location in which to save it.

The name of a Word document can consist of several words with spaces between the words, making it easier to understand.

Below: Giving your document a logical name at your first save makes it simple to find later.

Resaving Word Documents

While working on a Word document, it's worth saving the file every few minutes to avoid losing data if a computer problem occurs. This can be done in a variety of ways:

○ **Keyboard shortcut**: Press Ctrl+S. You won't see much happening (a floppy disk symbol may briefly appear), but the file will have been saved.

○ **Toolbar button**: Click on the Save button, which looks like a floppy disk, on the Quick Access Toolbar. The word Save will appear if you hover over it.

Hot Tip

Filenames can be quickly changed within your Documents Library. Just select a file, press F2 on the keyboard and type a new name for the file.

○ **Autosave**: Let Word take the strain. Go to the File tab and select Options at the bottom of the menu that appears. Click Save. Select the time interval between saves and a default location where you want Word to save the documents.

Above: You can personalize how frequently your Word document is autosaved.

Changing the Name of a Word Document

To change the name of a Word document, or save a copy with a different name, have the file open in Word. Press F12 and the Save As dialogue box will appear. Enter a new name and, if required, location for your Word document, then click the Save button. The new Word document will not overwrite the old one.

MOVING AROUND A DOCUMENT

It can be hard work to scroll through hundreds of pages in a document and find the text you are looking for. However, there are several shortcuts to save hours of searching.

QUICK MOVES WITH THE KEYBOARD

- **Ctrl+Home:** The cursor moves to the beginning of the document.

- **Ctrl+End:** The cursor moves to the end of the document.

- **Home:** The cursor moves to the beginning of the line.

- **End:** The cursor moves to the end of the line.

○ **Page up/down**: The cursor
moves up or down one whole
screen page at a time.

○ **Ctrl+down/up arrow**:
The cursor moves up or down
one paragraph at a time.

Hot Tip

When using the Ctrl key with another key,
always hold down the Ctrl key first before
pressing the other key.

SCROLLING

The scroll bars onscreen and the scroll wheel on the mouse can all be used to move quickly through a document.

Scroll Bars

The vertical and horizontal scroll bars will only appear onscreen when you hover your mouse over the scroll bar area.

Above: Hover over the appropriate area to reveal the scroll bars.

These scroll bars can be used as follows:

- **Drag the marker:** The scroll bar marker shows the current position in the document. Drag this marker to quickly move up and down or across the document.

- **Click next to the marker:** Scroll one screen page up, down or across by clicking next to the scroll bar marker, inside the scroll bar.

Above: Clicking on the arrows to scroll through your document is slower (and so more precise) than using the scroll bars.

- **Click on the arrows**: Click on the arrows (triangles) at the ends of the scroll bars to scroll up, down or across the document. This is one of the traditional techniques and the slowest method.

Check Where You Are

When dragging the vertical scroll bar marker, the page number to which you are moving will be displayed next to it.

Scroll Wheel

If your mouse has a scroll wheel, this can be used to move quickly around a document. If there is only one scroll wheel, this can be used to scroll up and down a document by rotating it. If there is a second scroll wheel, it can often be used to scroll across a document. Click the scroll wheel to switch on horizontal and vertical scrolling. The mouse pointer will change and can be moved away from the centre of the screen to begin scrolling. Click the scroll wheel again to switch this off.

Below: The page marker that appears next to the scroll bar means you know exactly where you are.

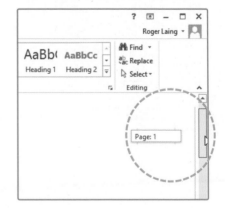

WORKING WITH DOCUMENTS

STARTING WITH A NEW OR EXISTING DOCUMENT

There are several approaches to creating a document in Word, and lots of time-saving techniques that can save hours of typing. The following section explains how to use blank documents, templates and existing files.

USING A BLANK DOCUMENT

When Microsoft Word is opened, a blank document is instantly created, making it quick and easy to start typing. However, there are some premade documents called templates that can save hours of typing.

What Is a Template?

A template is a ready-made document containing text, images and other information. It can save a lot of time and typing, and is useful for creating letters, faxes, expense claim forms and reports.

A template is similar to an original copy of a document, which can be photocopied time and time again without marking the original.

Where Are Word's Templates?

Word comes with a selection of templates, and many more are available online. To use a template, click the File tab on the Ribbon and select New. A dialogue box will appear showing the available templates. Select one and click Create in the window that opens.

Below: The premade templates can save you both time and effort, and are easily recognized.

Below: Example of a chosen template.

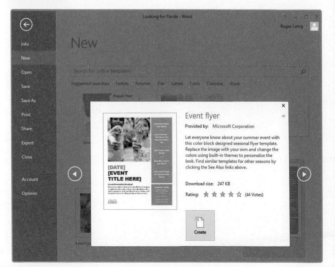

Hot Tip

The quickest way to get to the Open dialogue box is to press the Ctrl key and letter O.

USING AN OLD FILE

One popular method of creating a new document is to reopen an existing document and resave it with a different name. However, Word has a quicker solution:

○ Go to the **File menu**, select Open and locate the Word document you want.

○ **Right-click** on the file you want to copy.

○ From the pop-up menu, select **Open a copy**.

○ A **copy** of the document will be opened, leaving the original intact.

Below: Making a copy of a document will allow you to change certain aspects, while keeping the original just as it is.

TYPING AND FORMATTING TEXT

You can rapidly type text into a document in Microsoft Word, but changing how it's presented can take a lot longer if you don't know the techniques and shortcuts.

STANDARD SETTINGS

Word uses some default settings with new documents. Typically, it's an A4 portrait-shaped page with single line spacing, text aligned left, using the font Times New Roman or Calibri, size 11 (no longer 12), black. However, you can change these and many other settings.

CHANGING THE FONT, COLOUR AND SIZE

Common attributes, including the type of font, size and colour, can all be changed using the Home tab on the Ribbon.

Default Font Settings

Each Word document has a number of settings for standard text (known as Normal). It is simple to change these attributes, including the font, colour and size, by doing the following:

- Open the Font dialogue box by holding down the **Ctrl key** and pressing **D** on the keyboard.

- **Select** what you want to use throughout the document.

- Click on the button labelled **Set As Default**.

Above: Choosing the right font will make or break the presentation of your work.

ADDING BOLD, UNDERLINE AND ITALICS

While popular font attributes, such as bold, underline and italics, can be set via the Font dialogue box or Formatting toolbar on the Ribbon's Home tab, it's quicker to use keyboard shortcuts:

Hot Tip

Increase or reduce the size of a font by holding down the Ctrl and Shift keys, then pressing the > key to make the font size larger, or the < key to make it smaller. This also works for selected text.

- **Bold:** Ctrl+B.
- **Underline:** Ctrl+U.
- **Italics:** Ctrl+I.
- **Double underline:** Ctrl+Shift+D.

CHANGING ALIGNMENT

Use the Paragraph settings on the Home tab, or the following shortcut keys:

- **Left-align a paragraph:** Ctrl+L.
- **Right-align a paragraph:** Ctrl+R.
- **Centre a paragraph:** Ctrl+E.
- **Left- and right-justify a paragraph:** Ctrl+J.

If you change your mind, press the keys again to switch back to left-aligned.

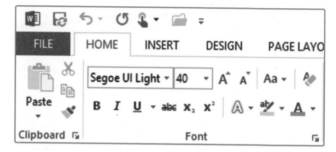

Above: Your font choices will always be close by in the Home ribbon.

Hot Tip

A quick way to change text to the default settings is to select it, and press the Ctrl key and space bar.

LINE SPACING

This is the spacing between each line of text in a paragraph (which is often different to the space before and after a paragraph if there is one). The following shortcut keys can be used to adjust it:

- ○ **Single**: Ctrl+1.
- ○ **Double**: Ctrl+2.
- ○ **1.5 lines**: Ctrl+5.

Below: Setting up line spacing to fit requirements is quite simple once you know where to look.

Paragraph	?	✕

Indents and Spacing | Line and Page Breaks

General

Alignment: Left

Outline level: Body Text ☐ Collapsed by default

Indentation

Left: 0 cm   Special: By:

Right: 0 cm   (none)

☐ Mirror indents

Spacing

Before: 0 pt   Line spacing: At:

After: 35 pt   Single

☑ Don't add space between paragraphs of the same style

Preview

Tabs...   Set As Default   OK   Cancel

PARAGRAPH PROBLEMS

Sometimes, Word will add an unwanted or extra-large line space before or after a paragraph. To change this, select the paragraph of text and right-click. From the shortcut menu that appears, select Paragraph to open a dialogue box. Under Spacing, change the values against Before and After to those you want.

SELECTING TEXT

If you can select text quickly, the time spent manipulating paragraphs and editing sentences can easily be halved. The following section shows the fastest methods to save time and ease frustration.

USING THE MOUSE

In most cases, the fastest technique for selecting text is to hold the left button down on the mouse and swipe the pointer across the text. However, there are other methods:

- **Double-click:** Double-click on a word to select it.

- **Triple-click:** Three clicks over a word will select the entire paragraph.

- **Click from the side**: Move the mouse pointer to the left of the page. When it changes to a white arrow pointing up to the right, left-click the mouse once to select the adjacent line of text.

- **Double-click from the side**: Do the same as above, but click twice to select the entire paragraph next to the mouse pointer.

- **Triple-click from the side**: Follow the same moves as above and click three times with the left button to select all the text in the document.

- **Ctrl+swipe**: Hold down the Ctrl key and swipe over some text to select it. Release the left button but keep the Ctrl key held down, move to some other text and select it. The first block of selected text will remain highlighted. Repeat this procedure to select more unconnected blocks of text.

- **Alt+swipe**: Selects part of a document, irrespective of content. Hold down the Alt key on the keyboard, then keep the left button held down on the mouse and move down and across the screen to select a section of the document.

Below: Click from the side to select an adjacent line of text.

Shift+click: Position the cursor at the beginning of the block of text you want to select. Move the mouse pointer (do not left-click with it) to the point in the text where you want to end the selection (you may need to scroll down the screen). Hold down the Shift key on the keyboard, then left-click once to select all of the text.

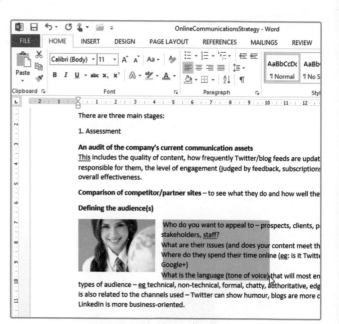

Above: Alt+swipe allows you to select very specific areas of a document, regardless of where words and lines start and finish.

USING THE KEYBOARD

The following keyboard shortcuts can save hours of editing time:

Ctrl+Shift+left/right arrow key: Selects a word to the left/right of the cursor.

Ctrl+Shift+up/down arrow key: Selects a paragraph of text.

Shift+Home/End: Selects all the text from the cursor to the beginning (Home key) or end (End key) of the line.

Ctrl+Shift+Home/End: Selects all the text from the cursor to the beginning (Home key) or end (End key) of the document.

Shift+Page up/down: Selects a full screen of text above (Page up) or below (Page down) the cursor.

Hot Tip

By far the quickest way to select all the text in a document is to press Ctrl+A.

DELETING, MOVING AND COPYING TEXT

Changing, deleting, moving and copying text are regular tasks within Word. These shortcuts enable you to save time when editing text.

DELETING TEXT

There are two keys – the Delete key and the Backspace key (above the Enter or Return key) – that, used with other keys, can remove large chunks of text.

Ctrl Deleting

Hold down the Ctrl key and press Delete once to remove an entire word. This deletes the word that follows the cursor. To delete the word before the cursor, hold down the Ctrl key and press the Backspace key once.

Select and Delete

In the previous section of this chapter are detailed instructions on quick techniques for selecting paragraphs and blocks of text. Once some text has been selected, press Delete on the keyboard to remove it from the document.

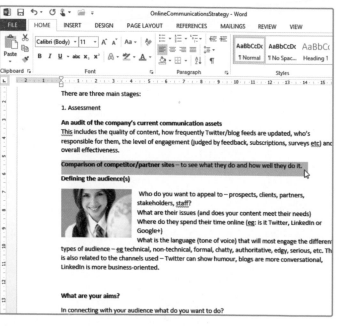

Above: Instead of erasing each letter separately, use the select-and -delete method to remove larger chunks of text in one fell swoop.

MOVING THROUGH TEXT

It can be very frustrating moving up and down a document using the keyboard, especially the arrow keys. However, there are some shortcuts:

○ **Ctrl+left/right arrow keys**: Hold down the Ctrl key and press the left or right arrow key to jump one word at a time.

○ **Ctrl+up/down arrow keys**: Hold down the Ctrl key and press the up or down arrow keys on the keyboard to jump one paragraph at a time.

○ **Home/End**: Moves the cursor to the beginning or end of a line of text.

- **Ctrl+Home/End**: Moves the cursor to the beginning or end of a document.

- **Page up/down**: Moves the cursor up or down one full screen of the document.

MOVING TEXT

Text can be quickly and easily moved along a line, to another paragraph or even to another document.

Cut and Paste

The most traditional method for moving text is to cut and paste it. This involves selecting the text, then doing one of the following to cut it (the selected text will disappear from the document, but will reappear when it's pasted):

- **Right-click**: Right-click the selected text and a shortcut menu will appear. Choose Cut from the menu.

- **Ctrl+X**: Hold down the Ctrl key on the keyboard and press the letter X to cut the selected text.

- **Cut toolbar button**: The Cut toolbar button looks like a pair of scissors and is on the Ribbon's Home tab.

Left: One way to cut text is to right-click the selected text and select Cut from the menu.

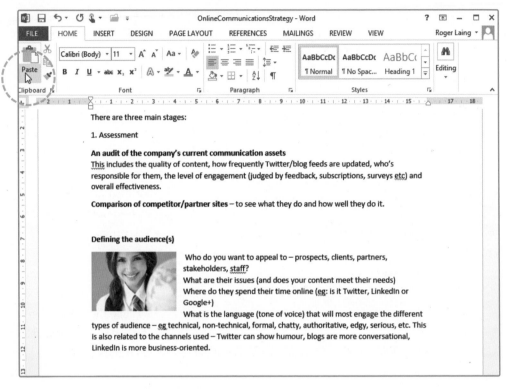

Above: One way of pasting text is to use the Paste toolbar button.

Fast Pasting Techniques

Pasting works in a similar way. To paste the text, right-click and choose Paste, press Ctrl+V or use the Paste toolbar button.

Dragging Text

Select the text and position the mouse pointer over it until it changes to a white arrow. Hold the left button down and move the mouse pointer to the new location for the text (you may see a faint vertical line). Release the left button and the selected text will move).

Hot Tip

To copy text when dragging it, hold down the Ctrl key (or 'Alt' on a Mac) and release the mouse button first.

Above: You can paste your copied material from the right-click menu.

COPYING TEXT

The methods for copying and pasting text are similar to cutting and pasting:

○ **Right-click**: Right-click the selected text and choose Copy from the menu. Right-click on the location where the text is to be pasted and choose Paste from the menu.

○ **Ctrl+C**: Press these keys to copy the selected text. Position the cursor where the text is to be pasted, then press the Ctrl key and the letter V.

○ **Copy button**: The Copy toolbar button looks like two pieces of paper and is on the Ribbon's Home tab. Click on it to copy the selected text. Position the cursor where you want the text and click Paste on the Home tab.

Above: One way of copying text is to use the Copy button on the Home tab of the Ribbon.

CHANGING THE VIEW

The onscreen view of a Word document can sometimes be difficult to scroll through, making it hard to find specific text. To make it easier, you can change the way you view pages.

WHAT YOU SEE IS WHAT YOU GET (WYSIWYG)

Print Layout is popular because it shows how each page will look when printed, including all four margins and the position of text, tables and images. To select Print Layout:

- **Print Layout button**: Click on the Print Layout button in the Status bar at the bottom of the Word window.

- **View tab**: Click the Ribbon's View tab and select Print Layout.

Above: One way of selecting Print Layout is to click on the button in the Status bar at the bottom of the window.

Below: To prevent being distracted by all of Word's features, your desktop or other documents, use Read Mode to stay focused – it affords a much 'cleaner' view.

FULL-SCREEN VIEW

Sometimes, you don't want access to all the features of Word, especially when text is being proofread. Consequently, it may be easier to hide all of these buttons and menus. This lets the text fill as much of the screen as possible. Click the View tab on the Ribbon and select Read Mode. To switch off the full-screen view, click on Close in the top-right corner.

OTHER USEFUL VIEWS

There are other views available in Word. Try them and see which you are most comfortable using:

- **Draft view:** This view hides the margins to show more of the text. Pages are divided by a faint dotted line.

- **Web layout:** Useful if a Word document is going to be converted into a web page.

- **Outline view:** Provides a list of the headings, which is helpful if you want to see the structure and content of a long document.

PRINTING

One of the most important aspects of word processing is printing. It's one of the functions of a typewriter, from which the word processor originates. The following pages cover the fastest techniques and typical problems that may arise.

PRINT PREVIEW

The best starting point when deciding to print a document is to see what it will look like before the printer starts to churn out the paper. While the Print Layout view of the document will help, it's best to use Print Preview as a final check. To access it:

Above: Print Preview is a necessary step to ensure that your document will be printed to your satisfaction.

Hot Tip

Hold down the Ctrl key and press F2 to open the Print Preview screen.

○ **File tab:** Click on the menu and choose Print.

○ **Quick Access Toolbar:** Click the icon of a page with a magnifying glass. If it's not showing, click the drop-down arrow beside the toolbar and select Print Preview and Print.

CHANGE HOW YOUR DOCUMENTS PRINT

Beside the preview of your page, you'll see the various settings that you can select to alter the way your document prints. These include:

○ **Print All Pages:** Or you can choose which pages to print.
○ **Orientation:** Which can be portrait or landscape.
○ **Size:** Such as Letter or A4.
○ **Margins:** Alter the amount of white space around your document.
○ **Page Per Sheet:** Useful if you want to print a number of documents, such as your slide notes, on a single piece of paper.

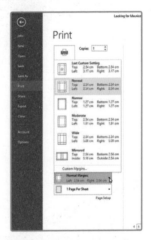

Above: To customize your margin before printing, make sure the setting is correct.

○ **Printer**: Select which printer you want to use. Click on Printer Properties and, depending on your printer, there may be other settings you can alter, including whether you print in black and white or in colour, or you can shrink the size of text to fit on one page.

TYPICAL PRINTING PROBLEMS

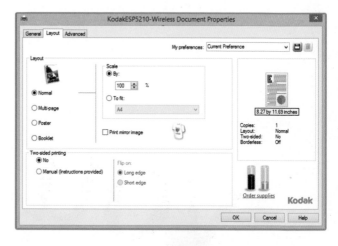

The following section outlines some of the common difficulties experienced when printing Word documents and how to resolve them.

Too Much White Space Around the Text

The result is you can use more paper than you need to print your document. To change this, go to Print Preview, select the Margins tab and adjust the top, bottom, left and right margins.

Above: Preferences, such as your chosen printer, can be set in Printer Properties.

I Only Want to Print One Page From A Document Containing Lots Of Pages

Make sure the cursor is positioned in the page to be printed, then press Ctrl+P. The Print dialogue box will appear. Click the arrow beside Print All Pages and select Print Current Page.

More Than One Page is Printed On Each Sheet of Paper

Open the Print dialogue box as above. Look at the bottom-left corner and the settings for Page Per Sheet. Make sure this is set to 1.

Above: Make sure Page Per Sheet is set to 1 if you don't want more than one page printed on a sheet.

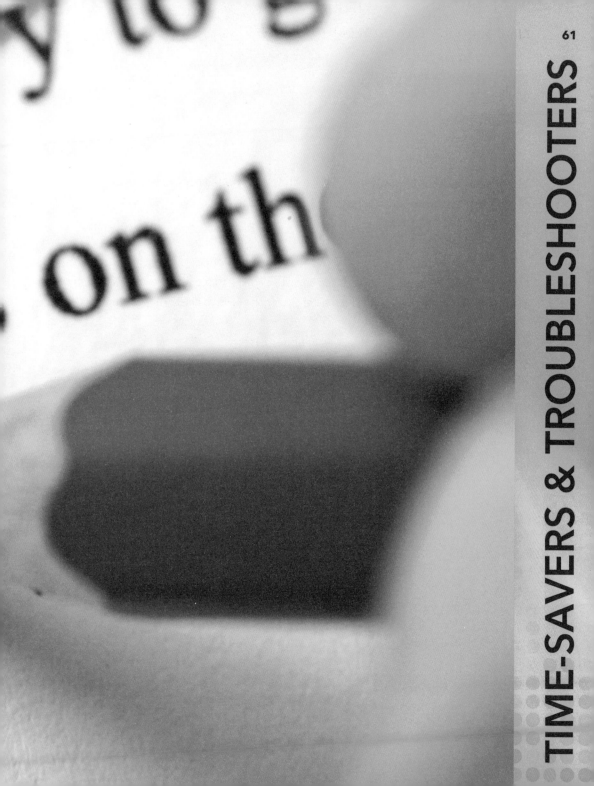

TIME-SAVERS & TROUBLESHOOTERS

TIME-SAVERS

There are several tools within Word that can help you type more efficiently and correct mistakes as they occur.

WRONG CASE

Press the Caps Lock by accident and it can be quite alarming to see several words or lines of text all in upper case across the screen. Fortunately, you don't have to delete the text and start again.

- Select all of the text that is displayed in **upper case**.
- Press **Shift+F3**.
- The text will change to **lower case**.

Above: Accidental Caps Lock happens to the best of us, but don't worry; instead of deleting your recently written sentence, use Shift+F3.

TWO CAPITALS

Hold the Shift key down for too long when typing a capital letter and the first two letters of a word will be displayed as capitals – for example, THe. If this happens, Word will automatically correct this mistake and change the second capital letter in the word to a lower-case letter. This is known as AutoCorrect and is covered in more detail later.

CAPS LOCK OFF/ON

Sometimes, the Caps Lock can be accidentally switched on, so when the Shift key is held down to type a capital letter, Word produces a lower-case letter instead. Luckily, Word recognizes this as a mistake. Not only does it swap the case of the word so that it starts with a capital letter, but it will also switch off Caps Lock.

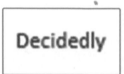

Above: Word will make sure you become aware of excessive Caps Lock ...

AUTOMATIC SPELLING CORRECTION

Word can automatically correct a number of typical spelling mistakes. For example, type the word 'thier' and it will be automatically corrected to 'their' after pressing the space bar or Return. This is known as AutoCorrect.

Above: ... and will change the words back to lower case for you.

I DON'T WANT TO AUTOCORRECT A MISTAKE

Sometimes, Word will try to correct a word that is right as it is. To reverse AutoCorrect, hover the mouse pointer over the corrected word until a small blue line appears. Move the mouse pointer over the line and a Smart Tag will appear. Click on this tag and you'll see some options for reversing the correction.

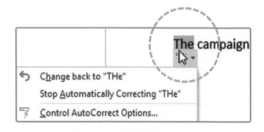

Above: If you have been corrected, but don't want the correction, do not despair; just hover over the word and choose from the options.

CUSTOMIZING AUTOCORRECT

You can change Word's AutoCorrect settings. To do so, click the File tab on the Ribbon, then select Options. In the dialogue box that opens, select Proofing and then click the AutoCorrect button.

Corrections and Exceptions

The dialogue box that opens has a tick-box list of corrections that can be switched on or off. If there are some words and abbreviations that require two

Hot Tip

The copyright, registered and trademark symbols (©, ® and ™) can be automatically created using AutoCorrect by typing in their respective letters in brackets. So, © is created by typing (c).

Below: You can personalize your AutoCorrect options if you have certain words you want spelled in a certain way.

Word Options	? ×

General	ABC✓ Change how Word corrects and formats your text.
Display	
Proofing	**AutoCorrect options**
Save	Change how Word corrects and formats text as you type: **AutoCorrect Options...**
Language	
Advanced	**When correcting spelling in Microsoft Office programs**
Customize Ribbon	☑ Ignore words in UPPERCASE
Quick Access Toolbar	☑ Ignore words that contain numbers
Add-Ins	☑ Ignore Internet and file addresses
Trust Center	☑ Flag repeated words
	☐ Enforce accented uppercase in French
	☐ Suggest from main dictionary only
	Custom Dictionaries...
	French modes: Traditional and new spellings ∨
	Spanish modes: Tuteo verb forms only ∨
	When correcting spelling and grammar in Word
	☑ Check spelling as you type
	☑ Mark grammar errors as you type
	☑ Frequently confused words

capital letters at the beginning (for example, ID), or that should be displayed in lower case (for example, mph), then these can be added to an exceptions list.

Spelling Corrections

Words such as 'Reveiw' are automatically changed to 'Review' if they are in the list in the AutoCorrect dialogue box. This list of typical errors is alphabetically sorted.

Removing AutoCorrect Spelling Corrections

You can remove an AutoCorrect spelling correction from the list by selecting it, then clicking on the Delete button. If you accidentally delete the wrong one, click on the Add button and it will be immediately re-entered.

Adding Your Own AutoCorrect Spellings

Words that you frequently misspell can be added as an AutoCorrect entry, to help save time when typing and reduce the risk of errors. Enter the misspelled version of a word in the left of the AutoCorrect dialogue box, under the label Replace. Enter the correct spelling in the box to the right. Click on the Add button and your entry will be listed.

Right: Make sure 'Replace text as you type' is checked, and then you can add in your own commonly misspelled words for Word to automatically correct.

Above: It is possible to customize your AutoFormat options.

AUTOMATIC FORMATTING

Open the AutoCorrect dialogue box and select the AutoFormat tab to see a variety of options for automatically formatting text as it is typed. For example, a website address can be converted into a hyperlink, so it can be clicked on to open the relevant web page. There is also a tick box to ensure that fractions are automatically converted (so 1/2 becomes ½).

STORED WORDS AND SENTENCES

Word can store a wide range of words and sentences, which can be inserted into a document without having to type all of the words again. This is known as AutoText and can be customized to help save time when preparing documents containing standard text, such as legal disclaimers.

Add an AutoText Entry
AutoText entries can be used in every document:

- **Select the text** you want to add, which will be stored as a 'building block'.

- Go to the **Insert** tab, click the **Quick Parts** icon and select **AutoText**

- Click **Save Selection to AutoText Gallery**. The 'Create New Building Block' dialogue box will appear.

○ Add a unique **name** and **description**, then click OK.

Delete an AutoText Entry

To remove an AutoText entry:

○ Go to the **Insert** tab, click the **Quick Parts** icon and select **AutoText**.

○ Position the mouse pointer over the **AutoText** entry. Right-click and choose **Organize and Delete**.

○ A dialogue box will appear. Select the AutoText entry and click on the **Delete** button.

Hot Tip

A quick way to create an AutoText entry is to select the text to be used, then press **Alt+F3** on the keyboard. The 'Create New Building Block' dialogue box will appear.

Above: Creating AutoText will save you time if certain passages of text are used by you regularly.

IMPROVING YOUR TEXT

Word can check your text as you type, advising on your grammar or even helping you choose alternative phrases.

GRAMMAR DILEMMAS

Microsoft Word checks the grammar of sentences and displays a blue wavy line underneath words or phrases it identifies as problematic. To resolve the error, right-click on the underlined words. A menu explains the error and suggests an alternative. To use it, select the suggested answer and the text will be automatically amended. If you click Grammar, an explanation of what's wrong will appear in a panel on the right.

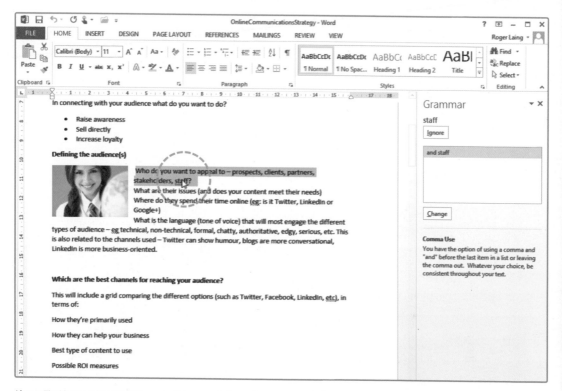

Above: The blue wavy line highlights a potential grammatical error. It is up to you whether you act on Word's advice.

Grammar Confusion

Sometimes, Word will find what it thinks is a grammatical error and provide a solution, when your sentence is correct. That's because Word doesn't understand colloquial expressions or instances where a word starts with a capital letter within a sentence. If Word wrongly identifies a grammatical error, the suggested correction can be refused by right-clicking on it and choosing Ignore or Ignore All.

Hot Tip

The blue and red wavy lines that appear underneath words for spelling and grammatical errors do not appear when the document is printed.

Find and Replace

Find	Replace	Go To

Find what: Catherine

Replace with: Kate

| More >> | | Replace | Replace All | Find Next | Cancel |

Above: To make changes in longer documents, Find and Replace will save you time.

CHANGE A WORD

If a particular word has been used throughout a document and it needs to be changed to something else (for example, a person's name is Catherine, but it needs to be displayed as Kate), then Word's Find and Replace can do this in seconds.

- ◉ Click on the Home tab and select **Replace**.

- ◉ Alternatively, press **Ctrl+H** to open the Find and Replace dialogue box.

- ◉ In the **dialogue box** that appears, enter the word or phrase to find and what it should be replaced with.

- ◉ Click the **Replace All** button to change all instances. (Though it is advisable to use 'Replace' initially to check you are not replacing text that shouldn't be changed!)

I NEED ANOTHER WORD

Sometimes, you can't think of another word to use with the same meaning. Word can save the day with its built-in thesaurus.

- ◉ Right-click on the word and choose **Synonyms**.

- ◉ A submenu will appear with some suggestions to **select**.

- ◉ Alternatively, click on **Thesaurus** and a panel will appear with further options.

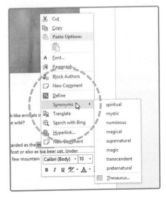

Above: Right-click on a selected word to see helpful suggestions for synonyms.

KNOW YOUR DOCUMENT DATA

If a document has to be written with a maximum or minimum number of words or pages, Microsoft Word can quickly help to keep track of this information and display it onscreen.

COUNTING WORDS

Word counts are useful for making sure your document is the right length. Word displays the total number of words in a document or in a selected block of text, in the status bar at the bottom of the page. When part of the text is selected, the word count for that selection is displayed, followed by the word count for the entire document (for example, 5 of 1250 means there are five words in the selected text and 1,250 words in the whole document).

HOW MANY PAGES?

The number of pages within a document is displayed in the bottom-left corner of the screen along with the page number that is currently on the screen. For example, Page 2 of 4 means the second page out of a total of four is currently onscreen.

MORE DETAIL

You can also see the word count of a document or selection by selecting that option from the Tools menu. This will also display totals for the number of pages, characters, lines and paragraphs.

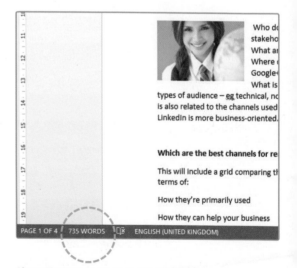

Above: The word count is displayed at the bottom-left corner of the document.

CHECKING FOR CHANGES

When a Word document is edited by you or someone else, it's often useful to know what has been changed or what was originally written. Word can show the differences using Track Changes.

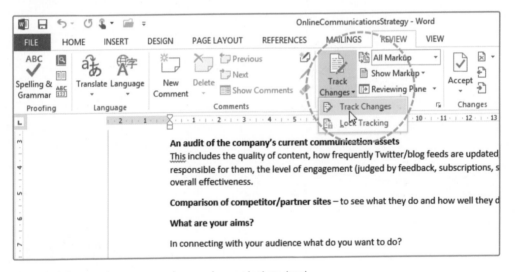

Above: Track Changes makes it easy to see where your document has been altered.

You can switch Track Changes on and off by holding down the Ctrl and Shift keys and pressing E. It's particularly useful if a document is edited by someone else and returned to the original author to review those changes. Any text that has been deleted, added or changed is displayed in different colours.

TRACK CHANGES

This can show all the edits that have been made to a document.

Switching On Track Changes

○ Click the **Review** tab and select the **Track Changes** button.

○ The button is **highlighted**, indicating Track Changes is on.

○ Try changing some text in the document, deleting a word or adding new text. All of these changes will be **displayed in a different colour**.

○ Deleted text will either remain onscreen with a **line through it** (strikethrough) or disappear from the screen, but a **message box** will be displayed to the right.

○ Click on the **Track Changes** button again to switch the feature off.

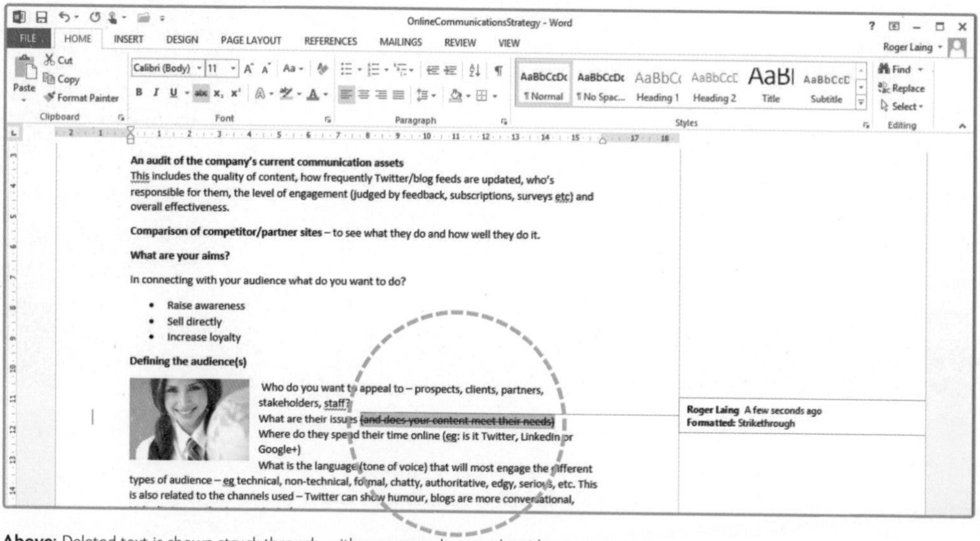

Above: Deleted text is shown struck through, with a message box on the side.

Checking a Document with Track Changes

The Reviewing pane (click on the Review tab and select Reviewing pane) lists all of the changes made to a document in a panel on the left.

Changing the Colours and Track Changes Features

The colours used in Track Changes when deleting, adding and editing text can be altered. Click the arrow in the corner of the Track Changes section of the Review tab, then select Advanced Options from the dialogue box that opens.

Accepting and Rejecting Changes

Individual changes can be accepted or rejected by right-clicking each one and choosing the appropriate option from the menu.

Comparing an Original And Amended Document

If Track Changes does not work or a document is amended, but you still have the original, then Word can compare two documents and highlight the differences. Click the Review tab and the Compare button. A small dialogue box will appear. Locate and choose the two documents to compare, and customize how the differences are displayed.

Above: In the Advanced Options box you can customize colours and styles to make changes more obvious.

> ## Hot Tip
> If several people edit a document, all of the changes can be reviewed. Click Compare on the Review tab and select Combine.

Above: You can set up the document to limit the changes that others can make.

CONTROLLING CHANGES

Word can restrict what edits can be made to a document. Click the Review tab and the Restrict Editing button. A list of options is displayed on the right. You can apply formatting and editing restrictions as well as specify rights for certain users.

COMMENTING ON A DOCUMENT

Another approach to editing a document is to add comments throughout the text that are displayed to the side of or below the document.

Inserting a Comment

Position the cursor where the comment needs to be added, click the Insert tab and choose Comment or click on the Review tab and select the New

Above: As well as tracking formatting and editing changes, it is possible to add comments to a document to explain changes.

Comment button. A comment window will open, either at the bottom of the screen or to the right. Add your comment and a marker will appear in the text. When finished, click the main part of the text to continue editing.

Reading Comments

If a comment within a document appears only as a marker, try hovering the mouse pointer over it and the entire comment may be displayed onscreen. Otherwise, try right-clicking on the comment and choosing Edit Comment. The Review tab also has a number of buttons to help you read each comment and show them onscreen.

Deleting Comments

Right-click on the comment and choose Delete, or use the button on the Review tab.

Above: When a comment is no longer needed, it is easily deleted. One way is to use the Delete button on the Review tab.

TYPICAL PROBLEMS

Problems can occur in Word, just like any computer program. While some may be user error, others are problems in the software. Here are some typical troubles you may experience and how to resolve them.

FORMATTING DILEMMAS

Early versions of Word gained a reputation for seemingly changing the font and size of text without warning. Although better now, there can still be formatting issues, which are usually easily resolved.

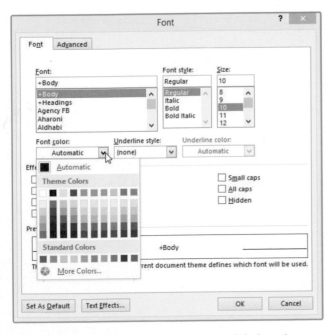

Above: Check the font colour is not the same as the background.

I Can't See The Text I'm Typing

The font colour is probably the same as the page colour. Press Ctrl+D on the keyboard and a Font dialogue box will appear. Look at Font color and make sure it's not the same as the page colour.

Text Keeps Changing to Bold or Another Font and Size

This usually happens at the bottom of the text. One quick fix is to hold down the Ctrl key when typing and press the space bar. This will switch off the Bold formatting and restore the default font settings.

When I Press Return, the Line Spacing is Too Big

Select the text affected, right-click and choose Paragraph, then change the settings for Spacing Before and After.

Font Settings Are Wrong When I Create a New Document

Press Ctrl+D on the keyboard to open the Font dialogue box, then choose the correct font settings and click on the Set as Default button. All future new documents will use these font settings (a message box may appear asking you to confirm these changes).

Above: To change the formatting of selected text, such as line spacing, right-click and choose Paragraph.

SCREEN DISPLAY ISSUES

The layout of the screen and its contents can sometimes be displayed incorrectly – or differently to how you expect it. Here are some of the typical problems that can arise and how to fix them.

There Are Dots Between Words, and Markers at the End of Some Lines

These markers indicate spaces and ends of paragraphs onscreen. Although not visible if the document is printed, they can be distracting. To switch them off, use the Show/Hide button on the Home tab. Alternatively, press Ctrl+Shift+8 (Cmd+8 on the Mac).

Below: 'Nonprinting characters' such as space markers and paragraph returns can be turned on and off using the Show/Hide button.

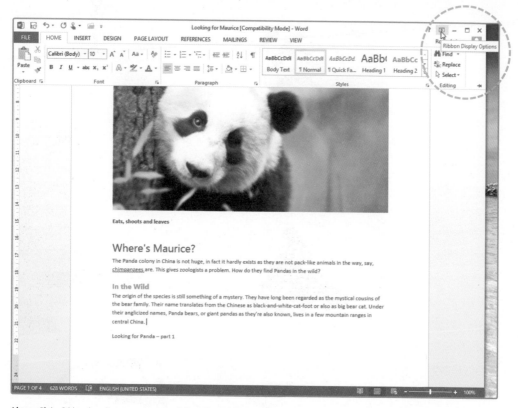

Above: If the Ribbon has disappeared, it is easily found again with a click on the box icon containing the upward-pointing arrow.

The Ribbon is Missing

Look for the icon of a box with an upward-pointing arrow at the top of the Word window. Click this and you can select to show the tabs again or the complete Ribbon with tabs and commands.

FILE TROUBLE

Word documents can disappear from the screen, refuse to open in later versions of the program and display worrying warnings about compatibility. Here are some common problems and solutions.

Where are the Documents I've Just Opened?

When two or more Word documents are opened, some of them may not be visible on screen, although they are still open. Click on the View tab and click the Switch Windows button to see a list of the Word documents that are currently open.

Word Cannot Open a File

- **Different file format**: If a file has been created in another program, then its file format (the type of file it is) may be incompatible. Return to the program in which the file was created and try to see if it can be saved as a Word document or something similar (.rtf, .txt).

○ **Later version:** Word documents created in Word 2013 will have a .docx extension at the end of their filename. Some early versions of Word cannot open these files unless they are re-saved as a Word 97–2003 type. To do so, choose Save As from the File tab and select the correct option from the 'Save as type' drop-down menu.

Hot Tip

Hold down the Alt key on the keyboard and press the Tab key to switch between programs and files.

Above: Resaving your file as a Word 97–2003 document can be helpful if you plan to send it to someone with an older version of Word.

NOVELS TO THESES

Microsoft Word's word processing capabilities are very sophisticated, and extremely useful once mastered. Here are a few examples of what you can create.

WRITE A BOOK

Word is capable of managing a document containing thousands or hundreds of thousands of words. It can display word counts, organize chapters with headings and subheadings, create a contents list and index, and automatically update footnotes. Whether a book is fact or fiction, Word can help with its creation.

BUSINESS REPORTS

Reports for work can often be complicated, with sales information from other sources, charts and accounting data. Word can store a vast assortment of information from other sources in a single document. It also has features to create charts or tables, add calendars and insert images to help further enhance a report.

UNIVERSITY DISSERTATION OR THESIS

Large and complicated assignments such as a 15,000-word dissertation can be created in Word and many of its time-saving features can be used. Footnotes, references, indexes and a contents page can all be created and automatically updated whenever changes are made or new text is added. Word counts are quick to display for the entire text or parts of the document, and when the completed masterpiece is ready to be professionally printed and bound, it can be emailed directly to a printer.

CREATE A PDF

The Portable Document Format (PDF) is a popular type of file that can be shared around the world and opened by most computers. Later versions of Microsoft Word can save a document as a PDF.

MAKE A WEB PAGE

A document created in Word can be saved as a web page and viewed using a web browser such as Internet Explorer, Google Chrome or Mozilla Firefox. If you are new to creating websites and would like to produce a web page, Word is a good starting point.

FILL IN A FORM

Save time at work by creating expenses claim forms, questionnaires and other official documents in Word. Columns of numbers can be totalled for adding up expenses and tick boxes can be included against options in questionnaires.

Below: You can make several different kinds of form, for example a checklist.

POSTERS AND LEAFLETS

Word can produce anything from a 'for sale' notice to an advertisement for a school fête to be printed on a variety of different-sized paper. WordArt, page borders, images and photographs can all be added to help illustrate the document.

POSTERS

Step-by-step:
Create a Poster

1. Press Ctrl+N to create a new document. Word will usually create an A4, portrait-orientated page. To change this, click on the Page Layout tab and select the Orientation button or Size button to alter as necessary.

2. To add a colourful border, click the Design tab and select Page Borders. Choose the type of border, style, colour and width you want from the dialogue box that appears and click OK.

    Right: Borders are fun on posters, and easy to customize.

Hot Tip

A page border can be removed by returning to the Borders and Shading dialogue box and selecting None.

3. Create an eye-catching heading for the leaflet or poster using WordArt. Click the Insert tab, then the WordArt button. Choose your WordArt style, type your text and click OK.

4. Type your text using bold fonts and colours. Add some text boxes from the Insert tab to list information such as contact or event details.

5. Images will give impact. Click the Insert tab and select the Picture button (for images on your computer) or the Online Pictures button (for Clip Art). Locate your image and insert it. If necessary, resize it by using the mouse pointer to click and move the small squares or circles around the box.

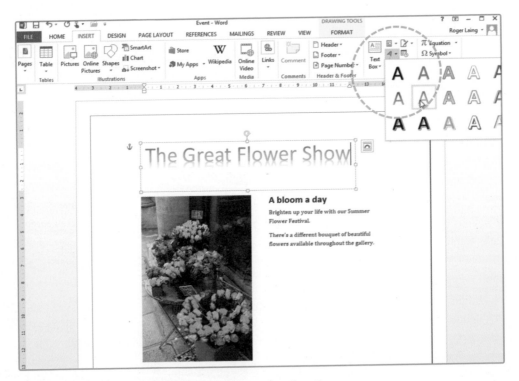

Above: To make your poster stand out even more, WordArt is an easy decorative option.

6. Save the document and, when you're ready, print it.

NEWSLETTERS

You don't need to learn the technicalities of desktop publishing with Word to be able to create a newsletter. Multiple columns, borders and images can all be created in a newsletter format using Word.

Above: Formatting a newsletter won't take you long, as columns, borders and images can all quickly be created in Word.

LETTERHEADS

Your address, the current date and a signature can all be created and included in a letter that can be reused and changed time and time again. Word can save hours of typing your address and any frequently used paragraphs of text. Just type it once and it's saved for using again in the future.

Step-by-step: Create a Letterhead

1. A letterhead should only contain text and images (for example, a company logo) that will appear in every letter. For example, your address, a greeting line such as 'Dear Sir' and a closing sentence followed by 'Yours faithfully' and your name.

2. Press Ctrl+N to open a new blank document, enter your address details on the right-hand side of the page (click the Align Text Right button on the Home tab). If you also want to show the recipient's address, then you need to create a table.

3. Click the Insert tab, select Table and choose Insert Table. In the dialogue box that opens, enter one row and two columns, then click OK. This creates a two-cell table.

4. Click the right cell, change the alignment to right, and enter your address (press Return on the keyboard to move down a line). The height of the table will grow as the address is typed. (The recipient's address will go in the left cell.)

5. Remove the border for the table so that it won't appear when a letter is printed. Click inside the table and a small cross should appear above the top-left corner of it. Click this, then select the Design tab on the Ribbon, then the Page Borders button. Select the Borders tab and choose No Border.

6. To add a logo to your letterhead, position the cursor where you want it, then click the Insert tab and choose Picture. From the dialogue box that opens, locate and insert your image.

Above: Insert a table to create space for your address and the recipient's address.

Hot Tip

When you need to use the letterhead in Word, click on the File tab and choose New, then locate the letterhead template.

Above: Remove the border from the table using the Page Borders button.

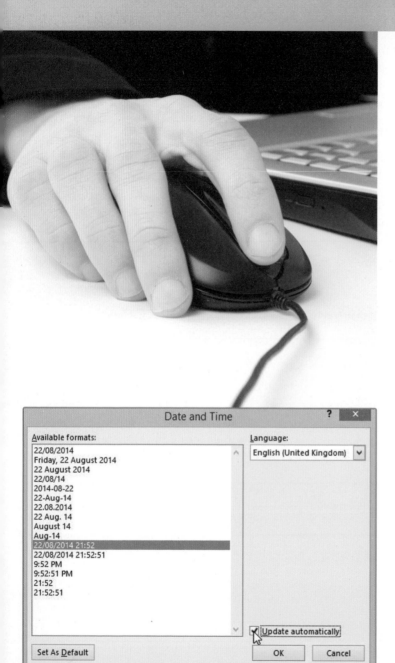

7. To resize it, select the image and a series of circles or squares will appear. Position the mouse pointer over these. When it changes to a double-headed arrow, hold the left button down and move the mouse to alter the size.

8. To insert a date that will be automatically updated whenever a new letter is created, move to the place in the document where you want it displayed. Click the Insert tab and select the Date and Time button. From the dialogue box that appears, select a date format and add a tick mark to the option labelled Update automatically and click OK.

Left: Use the Date and Time feature to automatically provide the correct date/time for each new letter.

Date and Time   ?   ×

Available formats: Language:

22/08/2014   English (United Kingdom)
Friday, 22 August 2014
22 August 2014
22/08/14
2014-08-22
22-Aug-14
22.08.2014
22 Aug. 14
August 14
Aug-14
22/08/2014 21:52
22/08/2014 21:52:51
9:52 PM
9:52:51 PM
21:52
21:52:51

                              ☑ Update automatically

Set As Default   OK   Cancel

9. Type your letter, adding a closing sentence, together with any relevant contact details (email address, direct line phone number).

10. Save the document as a template by changing the file type to a template in the Save As dialogue box. This will allow the letterhead to be used again and again without changing the original.

Hot Tip

If a table is at the top of a document and you want to insert something above it, click inside the top left-hand cell and press Return. The table will move down one line in the document.

Below: Save a letter as a template in order to use it again and again.

ADVANCED WORD

CUSTOMIZING THE RIBBON

You can modify Word to help customize the layout of the screen and display your most frequently used tools.

CHOOSE YOUR TABS

The Ribbon in Word is context-sensitive, so the tasks you do most frequently are gathered together into groups – such as the Font group or Page Background group – on different tabs. As everyone does not work in the same way, you can customize these tabs to suit you.

Adding and Removing Ribbon Tabs

- Click on the **File** tab and choose **Options**.

- From the dialogue box that appears, click **Customize Ribbon**.

- From the drop-down list underneath the heading **Choose commands from**, select **Main Tabs**.

- On the right, you'll see a list of the current tabs. Use the **Add and Remove** buttons in the centre of the dialogue box to include or exclude those you do or don't want.

Hot Tip

When dragging and dropping toolbar buttons, hold down the Ctrl key to copy them instead of moving them.

| Word Options | ? ✕ |

General
Display
Proofing
Save
Language
Advanced
Customize Ribbon
Quick Access Toolbar
Add-Ins
Trust Center

🖥 Customize the Ribbon and keyboard shortcuts.

Choose commands from: ⓘ

Main Tabs ⌄

Customize the Ribbon: ⓘ

Main Tabs ⌄

Main Tabs
⊞ Home
⊞ Insert
⊞ Design
⊞ Page Layout
⊞ References
⊞ Mailings
⊞ Review
⊞ View
⊞ Developer
⊞ NITRO PRO 9
⊞ Blog Post
⊞ Insert (Blog Post)
⊞ Outlining
⊞ Background Removal

Add >>
<< Remove

Main Tabs
⊟ ✓ Home
　⊞ Clipboard
　⊞ Font
　⊞ Paragraph
　⊞ Styles
　⊞ Editing
⊞ ✓ Insert
⊞ ✓ Design
⊞ ✓ Page Layout
⊞ ✓ References
⊞ ✓ Mailings
⊞ ✓ Review
⊞ ✓ View
⊞ ☐ Developer
⊞ ✓ Add-Ins
⊞ ☐ NITRO PRO 9
⊞ ✓ Blog Post
⊞ ✓ Insert (Blog Post)
⊞ ✓ Outlining
⊞ ✓ Background Removal

New Tab　New Group　Rename...

Customizations:　Reset ▼ ⓘ

Import/Export ▼ ⓘ

Keyboard shortcuts:　Customize...

OK　Cancel

Above: Choose the commands you want to add or remove from the Ribbon tabs.

ASSIGNING KEYBOARD SHORTCUTS

If you're familiar with using keyboard shortcuts (for example, Ctrl+S to save a document), then you can assign your own keyboard shortcuts to particular commands.

Add Your Own Shortcuts

Select Customize Ribbon from the Word options box as above, then click the Customize button beside Keyboard shortcuts. In the dialogue box that opens, select a category from the list on the left and a command to go with it from the list on the right. If a shortcut key is already assigned for this command it will be displayed. If not, click in the 'Press new shortcut key' box and press the combination of keys you'd like (there will be a message displayed if that combination is already in use), then click Assign to save the shortcut.

Hot Tip

If some buttons are missing from the Ribbon, open the Customize dialogue box, select the tab from the list and click on the Reset button.

Below: You can easily add or change keyboard shortcuts for your favourite commands by choosing to Customize.

Customize Keyboard

? ✕

Specify a command

Categories:

File Tab
Home Tab
Insert Tab
Design Tab
Page Layout Tab
References Tab
Mailings Tab
Review Tab

Commands:

Bold
BorderAll
BorderBottom
BorderHoriz
BorderInside
BorderLeft
BorderNone
BorderOutside

Specify keyboard sequence

Current keys:

Ctrl+B
Ctrl+Shift+B

Press new shortcut key:

Save changes in: Normal

Description

Makes the selection bold (toggle)

Assign	Remove	Reset All...		Close

DOCUMENT SECURITY

Word documents often need to have some level of security to ensure they are not edited by the wrong people or copied and used elsewhere. Some common security measures are outlined here.

SAVE WITH A PASSWORD

With the document you want to protect open, access the Save As dialogue box by pressing F12 on the keyboard. Click the arrow beside Tools, then select General Options. A second dialogue box will appear with options for entering a password to open the document and another password to modify it.

There is also a tick box for Read-only recommended, which will not allow anyone else to modify the document unless they save it with a different name.

DOCUMENT PROTECTION

Click the Review tab on the Ribbon and select the Restrict Editing button, which opens a box on the right of the screen. There are three steps to using this pane. The first provides formatting restrictions, the second limits editing, and the third switches on the editing restrictions with an optional password.

Formatting Restrictions

Select the tick box labelled 'Limit formatting to a selection of styles', then click on Settings below. A Formatting Restrictions dialogue box will open, allowing particular fonts to be selected. This is useful for a document which other people may edit using the wrong font.

Above: For important documents, password protection is an option.

Above: The Restrict Editing button is under the Review section of the Ribbon.

Editing Restrictions

Add a tick mark to the box labelled 'Allow only this type of editing in the document'. A drop-down list will appear underneath with options for tracked changes, comments, filling in forms and no changes (read only).

Exceptions (Optional)

Specific people can be selected to be able to edit the document freely. This feature is available where Word can communicate with a computer network and select users.

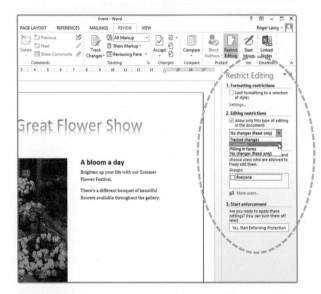

Above: Various ways to control your document are available in Restrict Editing.

PORTABLE DOCUMENT FORMAT (PDF)

Saving your Word document as a Portable Document Format (PDF) is a great way of protecting its formatting against changes. It is also a popular file type that can be shared around the world and opened by most computers using Adobe Reader, which is free to use, or similar software.

Step-by-step: Creating a PDF

1. Click the File tab, go to Export and select Create PDF/XPS.

2. Choose the location where you want to save it.

3. Click the Options button, select Document and uncheck the Document Properties box. This means that information about your document, such as when the file was created, by whom and when it was last changed, are not shared (see picture overleaf).

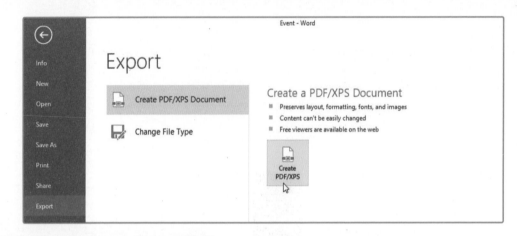

Above: Creating a PDF has never been easier.

4. You can save just part of a document as a PDF. In the Options box, specify the page range that you want to convert.

5. Click OK, then press the Publish button to create the PDF.

WATERMARKS

A watermark is useful for printed and protected documents (such as PDFs) for quotations, legal correspondence or helping to indicate a document is a draft or final copy. The watermark is a faint piece of text or image that's displayed across each page.

Left: Uncheck Document properties to ensure information about your document is not included in your PDF.

Inserting a Watermark

Click the Design tab and select the Watermark button. A palette of watermark styles with text will appear. If one of these can be used, select it. Otherwise, click on Custom Watermark and a Printed Watermark box will appear. If you're using an image (for example, a company logo), select Picture watermark and then the Select Picture button to find a suitable image.

If you want your own text as a watermark, select Text watermark, enter what you want to display and choose a font, size, colour and layout. Click OK to insert the watermark.

Removing a Watermark

Should you decide you no longer want the watermark – a draft becomes final, for example – click the Watermark button on the Design tab and select No Watermark in the box that opens.

Below: If the available watermarks don't suit your needs, you can create your own.

PRINTING ON TO ENVELOPES AND LABELS

Word can be used to print addresses and other text on to envelopes and labels to help produce professional-looking stationery.

PRINTING ON TO AN ENVELOPE

Click the Mailings tab and select the Envelopes button. In the box that opens, type a delivery address to print on the envelope and, if required, a return address (sender's address).

Below: Printing addresses on to envelopes looks professional.

Change the Envelope Size
Click the Options button to check the size of the envelope is correct. If it's wrong, click the drop-down list underneath Envelope size to choose the right one.

Change the Font and Position of the Address
In the Envelope Options dialogue box, click the Font button to change the type of font used. This can be for either the delivery or return address. You can also adjust the position of the text on the envelope using the From left and From top buttons.

Hot Tip

If your envelope size is not listed, choose Custom size and enter the width and height of the envelope.

Below: Customize the address position on the envelope to make sure it fits perfectly.

Envelope Options ? ×

Envelope Options **Printing Options**

Envelope size:

Size 10 (4 1/8 x 9 1/2 in)

Delivery address

Font... From left: 2.6 cm

From top: 3.9 cm

Return address

Font... From left: Auto

From top: Auto

Preview

OK Cancel

PRINTING LABELS

Word can print to a single label or create a sheet of labels with the same text on each one. Click the Mailings tab and select the Labels button. Under Address, enter the details plus any other text to appear on each label. Choose either Full page of the same label or Single label.

Change The Size of the Labels

- Click the **Options** button and you'll see a list of different labels.

- Choose a **Label vendor** (Avery, Microsoft, Tico) and a particular label **Product number** (usually found on your box of labels).

Below: Label Options lets you select the label product you are using, ensuring everything fits perfectly.

○   If your labels are not listed, select the **New Label** button and enter the dimensions.

Creating a Labels Document

If you want to save a sheet of labels and print them again in the future, then use Word to create a label template. Select the type of label and enter the text to appear on each label or one label. Click the New Document button on the Labels tab of the dialogue box, which will close and open the labels as a Word document. This can now be saved, printed and printed again in the future.

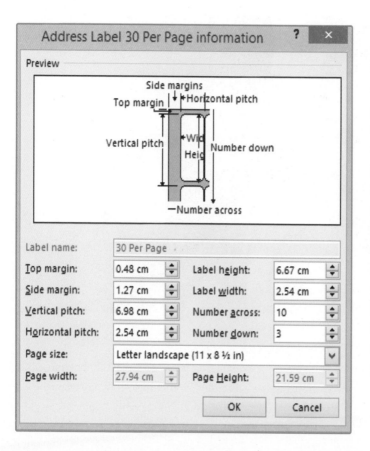

Labels Printing Incorrectly

One of the most common problems when printing labels is the text not being aligned with each label, so it typically prints across two. Get a ruler and check the dimensions of the sheet of labels are the same as those set up in Word. To do so, go to the Label Options box and click the Details button, which will bring up the dimensions for each label and the gaps between them.

Left: Make sure your labels match the dimensions set up in Word to avoid misaligned printing.

EDITING IMAGES

Most images inserted into a Word document can be edited to allow text to flow around or over them. Also, the brightness, contrast and colours used in an image, such as a logo, can be changed in Word to help improve its presentation.

ALIGNING TEXT WITH AN IMAGE

When an image is inserted into a document (for example, a photo, logo, diagram or chart), it is automatically put on its own line with text above and below. Sometimes, you may want the text to display alongside it. To do so, you need to change the text wrapping. Right-click inside the image and select Wrap Text. Choose one of the several options available, which include:

- **Square**: Wraps text around the border of the image.

- **Tight**: Wraps the text close to the image.

- **Behind Text**: Runs the text over the image.

- **Top and Bottom**: This is the default setting, in which the image is on its own line.

Above: You can choose to wrap your text around an image in several ways.

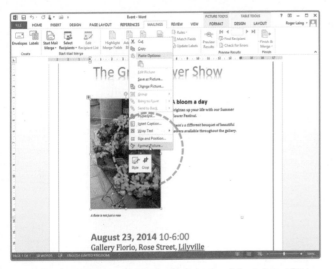

Above: To edit an image, right-click the image and choose Format Picture.

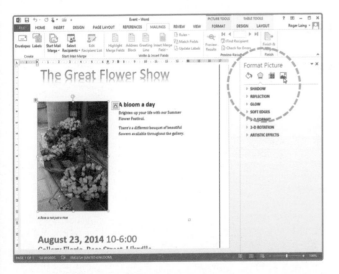

Above: From the pane that opens on the right of the window, select the Image icon on the right to find Picture Corrections.

ADJUSTING AN IMAGE

The brightness and contrast applied to most images, including drawings and photographs, can be adjusted in Word. You can also convert them to black and white or grayscale and adjust their size. These Picture Tools are available in the Format tab of the Ribbon, which appears when you select a picture.

Step-by-step: Adjusting Brightness and Contrast

1. Select the image that you want to edit.

2. Right-click inside the image and choose Format Picture to open a pane on the right.

3. Select the Image icon on the right and then Picture Corrections.

4. Under Brightness/Contrast, click on Presets and you'll see your picture with various combinations of brightness and contrast applied.

5. If none of those suits you, drag the individual sliders for brightness and

contrast, or use the arrow buttons to alter the settings. Any changes will be reflected in the main image.

6. To go back to the original settings, simply click the Reset button. Alternatively, click the X in the corner to exit the Format Picture pane.

Sharpen and Soften A Photograph

Select the photograph and the Picture Tools Format tab will open with a number of buttons across the top. Click the Corrections button and a palette of images will appear that shows the preset settings for softening or sharpening your photo, as well as Brightness/Contrast.

Convert to Black and White

Select the image and check that the Picture Tools Format tab is open. Click the Color button and, from the palette of options that appears, go to the Recolor section and select Grayscale for the most natural looking black-and-white effect. The image can be changed back to colour by returning to the appropriate menu.

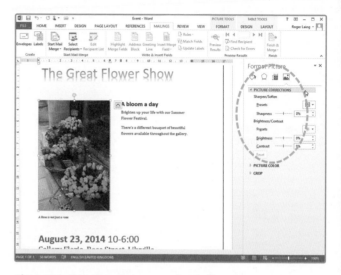

Above: Under Picture Corrections, you can adjust the Sharpness, Brightness and Contrast of your image.

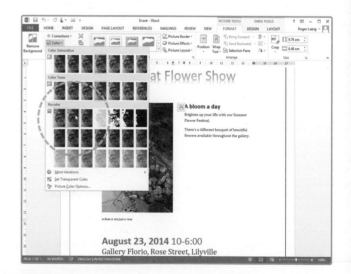

Above: Change your picture to black and white by clicking the Color button on the Picture Tools Format tab and choosing from the palette.

CROPPING AN IMAGE

If only part of an image needs to be included in a document, or it needs trimming to remove any unwanted space around the edges, then it can be cropped. This is not the same as resizing an image.

Cropping Options

Select the image and make sure the Picture Tools Format tab is displayed along the top of the screen. Click the drop-down arrow underneath the Crop button and a number of cropping options will appear.

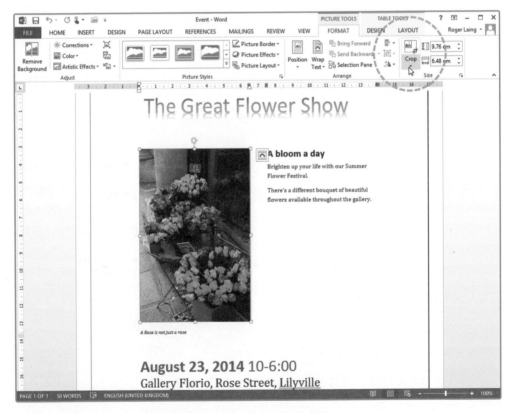

Above: Cropping a picture to show a required portion is made simple with the Crop tool.

○ **Crop**: Allows manual cropping. Position the mouse pointer over the crop markers at the corner or edges of the image. When the mouse pointer changes to a 'T' shape or '<' shape, hold the left button down to move into the image and crop a corner or edge. Release the left button to stop cropping.

○ **Crop to shape**: Allows the image to be changed to a shape, such as a round box, circle or heart shape.

○ **Aspect ratio**: Provides a list of preset ratios for width and height (most photographs use an aspect ratio of 3:2).

> ## Hot Tip
>
> **Depending on your image type, Drawing Tools may appear on the Format tab when you want to alter it instead of the Picture Tools used for editing photos.**

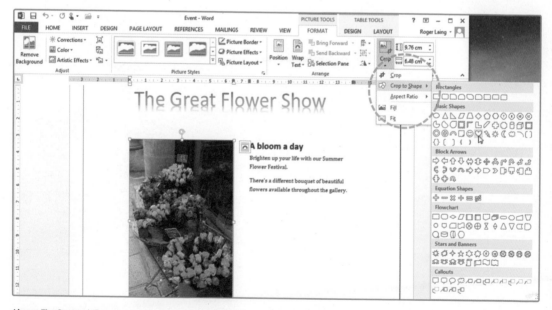

Above: The Crop tool allows you to crop your image into a wide choice of different shapes.

WORD ON THE GO

MOBILE WORD

Just because you're not by your PC, that doesn't mean that you can't still access your Word documents. Now there are versions of Word that will run on most tablets and smartphones, as well as through the browser on any PC or mobile device.

USING WORD ON YOUR TABLET

The lightweight nature of most tablets make them ideal for working with your Word documents on the go, particularly as the Word apps available will have most, if not all, of the features of the desktop version.

Above: Word on a tablet isn't much different to Word on a computer.

Windows Tablets

These run the same version of Word 2013 as you have on your desktop.

The only difference is that the buttons on the Ribbon are slightly larger and more spaced out for easier clicking by fingertip rather than mouse pointer.

Hot Tip

Although there's no Microsoft version of Word for Android tablets, like the Samsung Galaxy Tab, there are plenty of third-party apps available which offer many of the same, if not more, features.

iPad

There's a custom-made version of Word for the iPad. While it's free if you only want to read your Word files on the iPad, you have to subscribe to Office 365 to create or edit documents.

The Ribbon on the iPad looks more like a traditional toolbar.

Above: Tapping the Ribbon in Word for the iPad opens various drop-down menus.

Tap an icon on it and a drop-down menu opens with the various options. While it doesn't have the full range of features available in the desktop version, it has all the essentials to let you do most of the things you need to with your document.

WORD FOR SMARTPHONES

As part of Microsoft Office, Word is included in the Office Mobile app. The app lets you create, edit and save Word documents and is free for home use. For business use an Office 365 subscription is required.

- From your phone, you can **view, create and edit** your Word documents.

- As content and formatting are kept intact however you view your documents, they will **look the same** on your smartphone as on your desktop.

Above: Word on Android is easily accessible.

○ Some **basic format options** are available. For example, on an Android phone, tap Edit, then the More menu (three vertical dots), and select Format. Highlight the text you want to change and tap the format icon (the paintbrush). Now you can change font size, colour and add simple effects like bold and underline.

WORD BY TOUCH

Some of the latest features in Word are designed to work specifically with touch screens.

Touch Gestures

You can use the typical touch-screen gestures – including tap, pinch, stretch, slide and swipe – to zoom into documents or move between pages. Go to the Quick Access Toolbar and click the arrow beside the hand icon and select Touch. This spreads out the Command icons on the Ribbon so they're easier to use with Touch.

Read Mode

This opens your documents in a reading view, which minimizes distractions onscreen by closing the Ribbon and toolbars, leaving most of the screen to display your text.

Zoom In

Double-tap with your finger (or double-click with the mouse) and you can make objects in your documents – such as tables or pictures – fill the screen. Tap away from the object and it will return to normal size.

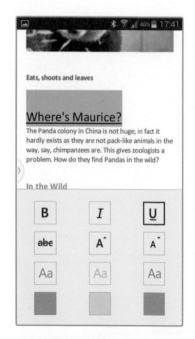

Above: You can edit basic font formats in Word on Android.

MICROSOFT WORD ONLINE

Part of Office Online, this lets you work on your Word documents through a browser on any PC or mobile device. To get started, go to Office.com.

○ You will need to **sign in** with your Microsoft account. Normally, you will have one if you use other Microsoft services such as Outlook (formerly Hotmail), or an Outlook 365 account you may have through work. There's also an option to sign up for a new account.

○ **Let's get started** offers you the option of creating a new blank document, browsing the templates or accessing a document you already have stored on OneDrive, Microsoft's file storage service.

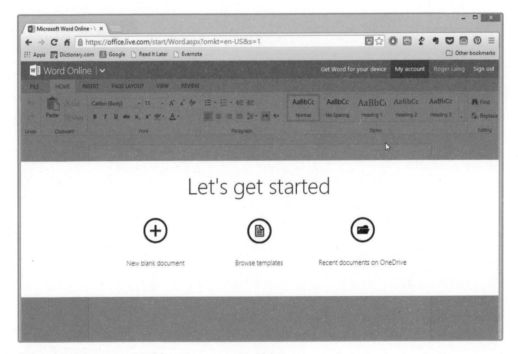

Above: After signing in, it is very straightforward to start using Word Online.

Hot Tip

Versions of the Word app are available to run on all Windows smartphones as well as the iPhone and some Android phone models.

- The Ribbon interface has **fewer commands** than the desktop version. But you can start your document online and then click OPEN IN WORD to send the document to your desktop version of Word and carry on where you left off.

- As you work on your document, Word **saves your changes** to OneDrive automatically. You'll see 'Saving...' or 'Saved' in the status bar at the bottom.

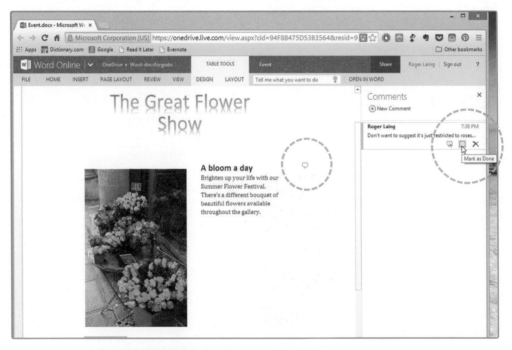

Above: Comments are indicated by a little speech bubble. Click on this to see the comment, reply and check the box when done.

- If there are **comments** in the document, a balloon/speech bubble marks where they are. Click to see the comment and reply to it. When you are finished, you can tick the box to show it's done.

- To **edit** the document, you have to be in **Editing View** rather than Reading View. Go to the View tab to change this.

- Once in Editing View, you can add or **change text and pictures**, alter the **layout** and change the **formatting**.

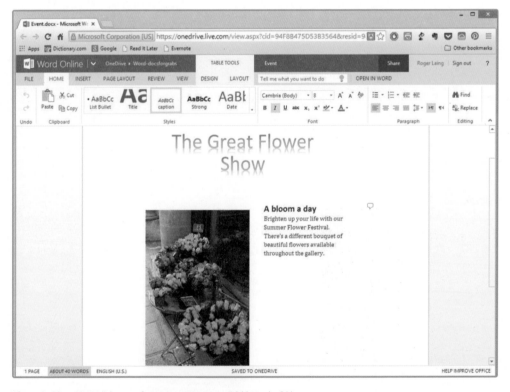

Above: In Editing View, all the main formatting options are available on the Ribbon.

○ There's no need to save changes, as they are **saved automatically**.

○ If you want to make some global changes and it's a long document, click the Replace icon on the Home tab, or type Ctrl+H, to open the **Find and Replace** box.

○ When you're ready, it's easy to **share your document**. Because it's stored online, you can just send a link to the people you want to invite to look at it. They can read it in their web browser or on their mobile device. Just press the Share button at the top of the page and fill in the details.

Above: Because your document is stored online, you can easily share it with others.

USEFUL WEBSITES AND FURTHER READING

WEBSITES

daiya.mvps.org/bookwordframes.htm
How to write a book using Microsoft Word.

http://msdn.microsoft.com/en-us/library/ff604039.aspx
If you want to look into using macros, this page introduces new programmers to using Visual Basic for Applications (VBA).

www.msofficeforums.com/word
Forum covering all Microsoft Office software, including a section for Word.

support.office.com/en-us
Microsoft's official website for help and troubleshooting, including past and current versions of Word.

https://store.office.com/appshome.aspx?productgroup=Word
App store for Word on the go.

FURTHER READING

Microsoft Word Expert Skills (Microsoft Official Academic Course), John Wiley & Sons, 2008

Duffy, Jennifer, *Microsoft Office Word 2010 Advanced: Illustrated Guide*, South-Western, Division for Thomson Learning, 2011

Hawkins, Rob, *Microsoft Word Made Easy*, Flame Tree Publishing, 2011

Lambert, Joan and Cox, Joyce, *MOS 2010 Study Guide for Microsoft Word, Excel, Powerpoint and Outlook*, Microsoft Press, 2011

Negrino, Tom, *Microsoft Office for iPad: An Essential Guide to Word, Excel, Powerpoint, and Onedrive*, Peachpitt Press, 2014

O'Leary, Linda I., *Microsoft Word 2010: A Case Approach, Complete*, McGraw Hill Higher Education, 2011

Pierce, John, *MOS 2013 Study Guide for Microsoft Word Expert (MOS Study Guide)*, Microsoft Press, 2013

Rourke, Claire, *Advanced Training for ECDL - Word Processing: The Complete Course for Advanced Word Processing and Microsoft Word in Windows XP and Office 2007*, Blackrock Education Centre, 2010

Tyson, Herb, *Teach Yourself Web Publishing with Microsoft Word in a Week*, Peason Education Ltd, 1995

Wang, Wallace, *Office 2013 for Dummies*, For Dummies, 2013

Wempen, Faither, *Microsoft Word 2010 in Depth*, QUE, 2010

INDEX